BUGS

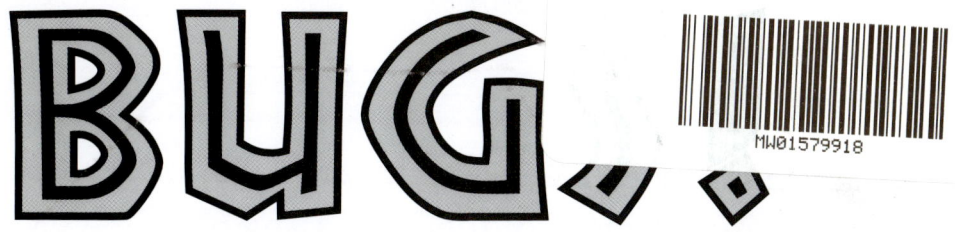

Written by Christopher Nicholas
Illustrated by Mike Maydak

Manufactured for Learning Horizons, Inc.
One American Road, Cleveland, OH 44144. Printed in China.
Fabriqué pour Learning Horizons, Inc.
One American Road, Cleveland, OH 44144.
Fabriqué en Chine.
Cover & interior design © 2001 Learning Horizons, Inc.

Visit us at: www.learninghorizons.com

They walk, crawl, swim, and fly all over the world. There are more of them than any other kind of animal on Earth! And they have been around for over 350 million years!

What are they?

(Hint: turn the page to find out...)

You probably call them bugs but scientists call them insects.

What makes an insect an insect?

For one thing, it has a special body. All insects have a hard shell on the outside called an **exoskeleton**. The shell protects the little insect just like metal armor protects a knight!

Ladybug

Earwig

Grasshopper

Ant

An insect's body also has three parts. It has a head, a middle section called a thorax, and an abdomen. These three parts are easy to see on one insect that everyone knows—the ant.

People have two legs. Dogs and cats have four legs—and insects have SIX! (Go ahead, count them!) But not all insect legs are the same. Some legs are good for jumping far. Others are perfect for climbing, grabbing, running, or swimming.

Grasshopper

Praying Mantis

Spiders have eight legs. They are NOT insects!

Dragonfly

Most insects have two or four wings. And just like legs, there are different kinds of wings. The dragonfly's big wings are perfect for flying fast and making quick turns in mid-air! But a beetle's wings are different—one pair is thick and leathery to protect the second pair of delicate flight wings.

Beetle

As you can see, bugs are a lot different from you and me. And speaking of "seeing," did you know that insects have two different types of eyes? An insect's **simple eyes**, called "ocelli," can only sense light. Their larger, **compound eyes** can see objects and animals and their movements.

Fly

A housefly's compound eyes have thousands of little parts called lenses. Each lens sees a piece of a bigger picture. What would an apple look like to a fly?

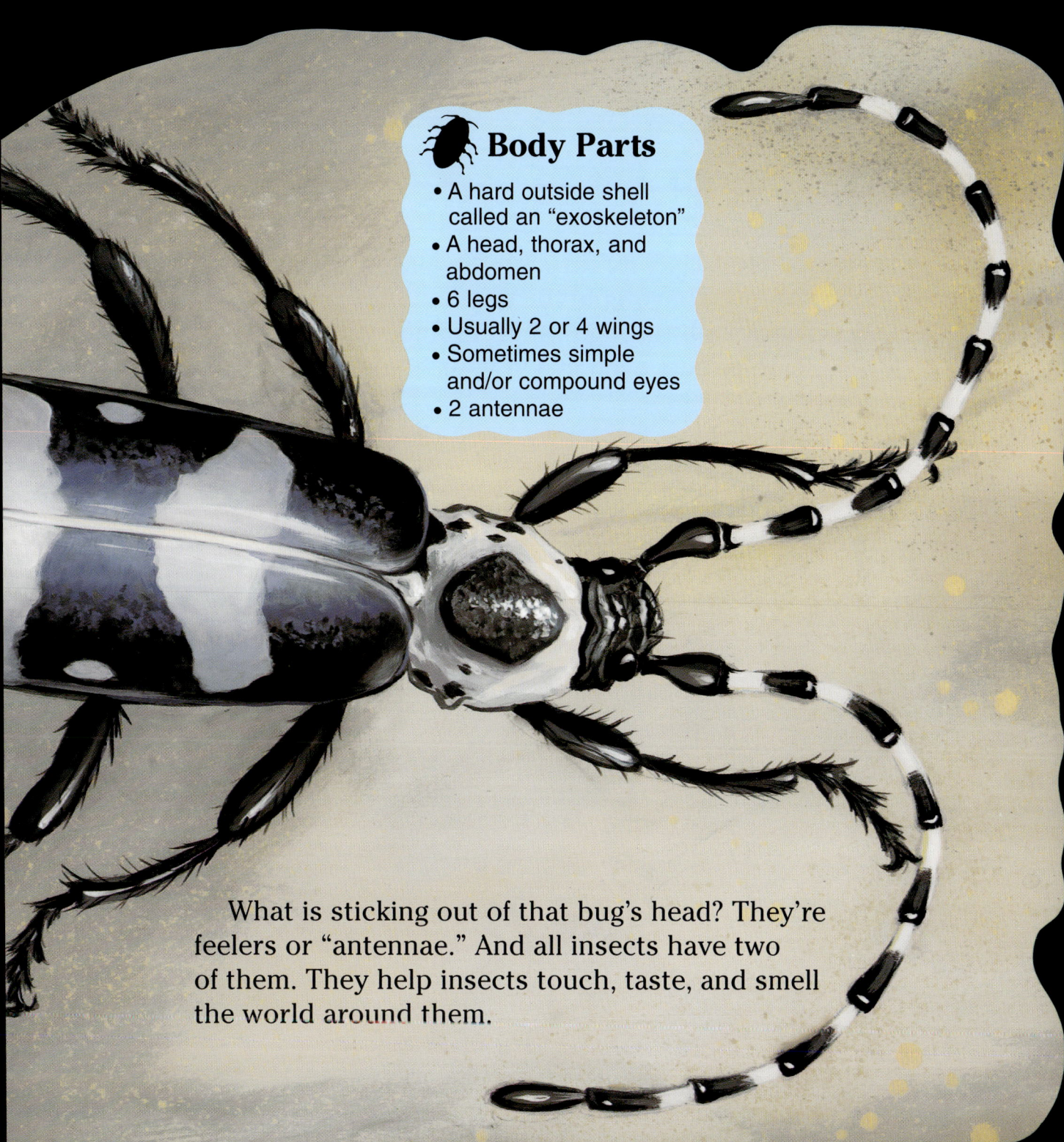

Body Parts

- A hard outside shell called an "exoskeleton"
- A head, thorax, and abdomen
- 6 legs
- Usually 2 or 4 wings
- Sometimes simple and/or compound eyes
- 2 antennae

What is sticking out of that bug's head? They're feelers or "antennae." And all insects have two of them. They help insects touch, taste, and smell the world around them.

Where do insects live?

Everywhere! They fly through the air and walk on the ground. They dig in the dirt and hide under rocks. They climb through the trees and swim in water. Some insects even live in your home!

Damselfly

Common stone fly

Harlequin bug with eggs

Waterstrider

Orange stone fly

Bees

People live together in groups called families. Some insects live together in groups, too. Ants, bees, and termites live in groups called **colonies.**

Ants

Where 🪲's Live
- In the air
- On the ground
- In dirt
- Under rocks
- In trees
- In and around water
- Some live together in colonies or hives

Termites

Each member of an insect group has a special job. Some find and gather food. Some build and dig. Others take care of the young.

Termites eat wood from trees—and from your house!

What do insects eat?

Some eat leaves and stems from plants and trees. **MUNCH!** Others suck nectar and juice from flowers and fruit. **SLURP!** And some insects like to eat other insects! **CRUNCH!**

Butterfly

Ladybug

Aphids

Ladybug larvae

Some insects drink blood from other animals—like you and me! **OUCH!** Other insects, like the cockroach and the fly, eat garbage, animal waste, and other dead things. **YUCK!** But they recycle garbage to keep the earth clean!

Mosquito

Fly

Cockroach

The little silverfish likes to eat paper. Keep him away from this book!

What 's Eat

- Plants
- Other insects
- Blood
- Wood and paper
- Garbage, animal waste, and other dead things

How do insects "talk" to each other?

Ants communicate through smells. They use odors to warn their nest mates of danger and to lead them to food.

Ants

Other insects send messages with movement! When a bee finds food, it will do a little dance in the nest to tell the other bees "it's time to eat!"

Bees

Many insects communicate with sounds. Male field crickets chirp by rubbing their wings together to attract a female cricket. Fireflies find each other with flashes of light!

Fireflies

How 🪲's "TALK"
- Smells and scents
- Motion
- Sound
- Light

Cricket

Wasp

How do insects protect themselves?

Wasps use poison stings to fight off predators. Other insects wear special armor.

Goldsmith beetle

Stink bug

How 🪲's Protect Themselves
- Stingers
- Hard shell or exoskeleton
- Bad smell
- Color

Giant walking stick

Scarlet and green leafhoppers

A few insects, like the stink bug, spray stinky liquids at their enemies. They are the skunks of the insect world!

Many insects have colors that blend with the places they live. This is called **camouflage**. Can you find the insects that color helps hide on this page?

How does an insect grow up?

All insects hatch from eggs. As they grow, they get bigger and begin to look more like their parents. (Just like you!)

Egg

Larva (Caterpillar)

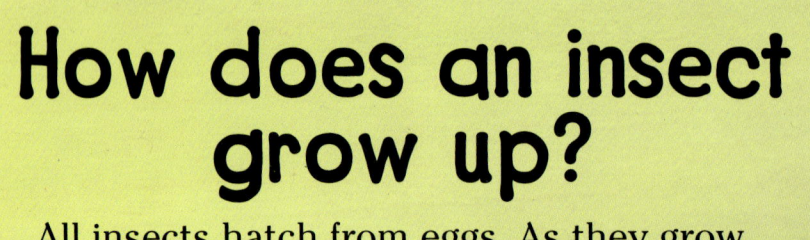

The change that insects go through from egg to adult is called **metamorphosis**. That's a big word that means "changes shape."

There are different kinds of metamorphosis. Some insects change by just growing bigger. Others grow wings. But there are some insects, such as butterflies, that change so much that the adult looks nothing like the youth.

Pupa (Chrysalis)

Adult

How 's Grow Up
- All hatch from eggs
- All go through metamorphosis

Bet you didn't know...

Flies can taste with their feet!

When in flight, a mosquito beats its wings 300 times in a single second!

The waterstrider can actually walk on water!

A flea can jump over 200 times its own length!

One ladybug can lay up to 1500 eggs in her lifetime!

Cockroaches are so smart that they have learned to run mazes in laboratories!

The giant water bug has been known to eat tadpoles and small fish!

A dragonfly can fly as fast as 30 miles (48 km) per hour!

Some bee hives have up to 50,000 bees!

Insects are amazing! But do you know what my favorite thing about them is? (Hint: turn the page to find out . . .)

A cricket can hear with its legs!